PLUG IN
&
STAY CONNECTED
TO

GOD

SYLVIA THIBODEAUX-PERRY

WESTBOW·
PRESS
A DIVISION OF THOMAS NELSON
& ZONDERVAN

Scripture taken from the King James Version of the Bible.

Definition in Chapter 4 taken from MacMillan English Dictionary 1

WestBow Press books may be ordered through
booksellers or by contacting:

WestBow Press
A Division of Thomas Nelson & Zondervan
1663 Liberty Drive
Bloomington, IN 47403
www.westbowpress.com
1 (866) 928-1240

ISBN: 978-1-4908-2176-4 (sc)
ISBN: 978-1-4908-2177-1 (e)

Library of Congress Control Number: 2013923721

Printed in the United States of America.

WestBow Press rev. date: 8/4/2014

IN LOVING MEMORY OF
MY MOM

AUGUSTINE TIZANO, THIBODEAUX
JANUARY 17, 1933 - MARCH 7, 2010

PURPOSE

Plug In and Stay Connected is a selection of stories to encourage you on how to get connected and stay plugged in to God. You can read some of the stories in the *Bible* today and realize that they are inspiration for your everyday life experience.

In this book, Sylvia shares with you how to go through life situations and come out victorious. She shares how to plug in and stay connected to God, no matter what you are faced with. She also emphasizes why it is important to stay connected.

Her passion is to encourage others and let them know that God is bigger than any situation or circumstances that one may face. We must never give up or disconnect (unplug) from God. He cares and loves us in spite of our faults or mistakes.

As you read this book, you will realize that getting connected to God gives you "Power" to maintain your love, joy, peace, hope, patience, strength, and faith in Him.

Leave your past behind. Be encouraged and know that you only go through seasons to come out.

ACKNOWLEDGEMENTS

The experience of writing this book has stretched me and my faith in God to grow in His Word and His ways. Thank you, my Lord and Saviour Jesus Christ, for drawing me to You. Thank you for your wisdom and knowledge that allows me to share your Word with others.

To my husband Curtis, and our three children Jonathan, Megan, and Raegan. Thank you for the love and joy you bring into my life. For believing in me, motivating me, and helping me grow into a better person.

Thank you for your time and patience, and most of all for having a listening ear. You all are greatly loved and appreciated.

To my dad (Ernest) and my late mother (Augustine), I am grateful for the morals and values you instilled in me and the firm faith foundation you gave me to build upon. I appreciate that you were there for me even when I went astray. Proverbs 22:6 KJV says, "Train up a child in the way he should go; and when he is old, he will not depart from it." Thank you both for a priceless foundation in the Word of God. I love you!

To my six sisters (Berthena, Barbara, Marilyn, Bernadine, Regina, Shirley) and one brother (Wyman). Thank you for being my friends as well as my siblings. For always being there for me and constantly reminding me to *"write"*… I love you all.

To my friends, thank you for words of encouragement. I love you.

Thanks to my Pastors, (Pastors whose ministries I've had the privilege of sitting under). Pastor Ronald and Drucilla Mayo, Bishop Harold and Ruby Vann, Pastor Happy and Jeanne Caldwell, Pastor Phil and Barbara Privette and Pastor S. Vincent Johnson. Thank you all for the impartation of the Word of God. A *special thank you* goes *to Pastor Mayo and Bishop Vann*, for the prophesy spoken over my life (confirming the exact words God spoke to me), "That I would be writing books." *I believe this is the first of many more to come.* Thank you all for believing in me and nurturing me and my family in the Word of God. I appreciate your prayers, words of encouragement, and most of all, for being men and women after God's heart. You all are a reflection of God's love and compassion. Again, Thank You.

CONTENTS

THE POWER
OF BEING
CONNECTED

CONNECTED:

Jesus (the son of the Living God), while on His journey stayed connected to His Father. Many times, He went off to a quiet place to pray. He had constant fellowship with God. Jesus was prepared at all times to face the enemy. He was endued with "Power" from on high. Like a lamp being plugged into an electrical outlet, it pulls forth a surge of energy, which brings forth the manifestation of light. Without the lamp being plugged in (or connected), there would be no light.

Therefore, our connection with God brings forth much **"energy and power."**

The *Bible* tells us in Luke 10:19 KJV, "Behold, **I give unto you power** to tread on serpents and scorpions, and over all the power of the enemy: and nothing shall by any means hurt you."

God is speaking to you and letting you know, if you live (abide) in me then, I'll live (abide) in you. There will be a "supernatural power" that passes your (man) abilities to do all things. You can live a life of freedom, abundance and power being connected to Him.

Let's look at the book of John 15:1-5 KJV, "I am the vine (connection), and my Father is the husbandman. Every branch in me that beareth not fruit he taketh away; and every branch that beareth fruit, he purgeth it, that it may bring forth more fruit. Now, you are clean through the Word which I have spoken unto you. Abide in me, and I in you. As the branch cannot bear fruit of itself, except it abide in the vine; no more can you, except you abide in me. I am the vine, you are the branches; He that abideth in me, and I in him, the same bringth forth much fruit; **for without me you can do nothing."**

Abiding means…to live or dwell, endure to be faithful to. **God wants you to know Him in a personal way.** He wants you to have an intimate relationship with Him. *Your love for God should be the motivating factor for your life.* If you want to know someone, you have to spend time with them and establish a relationship. (Examples: Naomi and Ruth, Mary and Elizabeth, David and Jonathan, Jesus and God). To know God, you must get into His Word and learn of Him (study and meditate in the Word), so you will know who He really is. You will find out that He is in control of **"ALL"** things.

Proverbs 16:1-4 KJV says "The preparations of the heart in man, and the answer of the tongue, is from the Lord. All the ways of a man are clean in his own eyes; but the Lord weigh the spirits. Commit thy works unto the Lord, and thy thoughts shall be established. The Lord had made all things for himself; yea, even the wicked for the day of evil." (*Punishment* will come for evil done).

You can make your own plans in life but, the final outcome is in God's hands. (You can prove that you are right but, is the Lord convince)? God weigh the spirit.

God wants you to trust Him. Trust God as if everything depended on Him. And work as if, everything depended on you. There must be a partnership between your efforts and God's control. The results are in His hands.

God created you for the purpose of fellowshipping with Him. We're not slaves or robots. (That's a lie from Satan). *God loves us so much that He gave each one of us a free moral "will."* It's up to you to decide if you would choose to love Him, as He is love.

DISCONNECTED:

The results of being disconnected: Let's look at Adam and Eve's life; for example. They took their free moral will and committed sin against God. This separated the relationship between God and Man.

It was never God's intention for us/man to know sickness, sin or death. When Eve sinned in the Garden of Eden, this opened the door for Satan to gain dominion over man. It also opened the door for the enemy (Satan), to steal everything that God intended for you and I to have and that includes your relationship with Him (God).

When your communion with God was severed, you lost not only your pure innocent mind toward God, but also the "knowledge" of how to handle or have a relationship with Him. Fear, doubt, unbelief, and distrust perverted the place where *revelation, wisdom and knowledge of God are intended to be.* Then, darkness came (something we would have never known or experienced). Satan brought along his relatives: envy, pride, jealousy and hatred. They came not only to destroy you, but to blind you from the truth of God's Will.

If you are not connected to God, there will be an absence of God's power. Therefore, Satan will come into your life and take possession of your mind and do whatever he chooses (things you never thought you would do). One thing I know for sure is Satan wants to keep you away from your destiny. I don't care what you try to do; you **cannot and will not defeat Satan without God and His Word.**

Now, I know what God meant when he said in Deuteronomy 8:3 KJV, "Man shall not live by bread only, but by every word that proceeds out the mouth of the Lord do man live." We need His Word to survive. (The Word of God feed our soul).

Remember, **Satan is a deceiver.** Satan comes to deceive, to destroy, and seduce you. He is also described as an angel of light (To trick you).

Matthew 24:4-5 KJV says, "And Jesus answered and said unto them, Take heed that no man deceive you. For many shall come in my name, saying, I am Christ; and shall deceive many."

(Be careful that no one misleads you into error).

2 John 1:7 KJV says, "For many deceivers are entered into the world, who **confess not** that Jesus Christ is come in the flesh. This is a deceiver and an antichrist."

Here are a few examples, in the *Bible*, where Satan deceived many. In the book of Genesis, Eve was deceived in the Garden of Eden by a serpent.

Genesis 12:11-20 KJV, Abram and Sarai deceived Pharaoh of Egypt and lied about his wife being his sister.

There are consequences for sin. Satan is a strategist. He plots, plans and schemes daily to steal, kill and destroy you.

Steal- Satan wants to take what is rightfully yours.

Kill- Satan wants to end your life.

Destroy- Satan wants to ruin and wreck you. He only wants to stop you from fulfilling your destiny.

C⟋

John 10:10 KJV says, "The thief, comes not, but for to steal, and to kill, and to destroy: I am come that they might have life, and that they might have it more abundantly."

Satan will deceive you into thinking you do not need God. Things may look like they are going well without God but, this is only for a moment/temporarily. Satan will bring sudden destruction into your life, when you least expect it. (he is subtle, crafty and devious). Living without the power of God brings frustration, anxiety, fear, doubt, worry, unbelief, bondage and slavery. You begin to feel hopeless, discouraged and maybe even defeated.

John 15:6 KJV says, "If a man abides **not in me,** he is cast forth as a branch, and is withered; and men gather them, and cast them into the fire, and they are burned."

Without the Word of God, the Power of God, and the Authority in Jesus' name, you will not be able to overcome the persecutions of the devil.

Psalms 34:19 KJV says, "Many are the afflictions of the righteous: but the Lord delivered him out of them all."

This is why it is important to Stay Connected to God who is our deliverer.

KNOWING GOD'S WILL FOR YOU

Do you know the Will of God for your life? Many pray for their selfish desires and gains to be met. Lord, give me this. Lord, give me that. (Seeking after His hands, instead of His face). We should be asking God to show us His Will for our lives and how to be obedient in what He wants us to do.

Matthew 6:9-10 KJV says, "Pray ye; Our Father which art in Heaven, Hallowed be Thy name. Thy kingdom come, **Thy Will be done** in the earth, as it is in Heaven."

Many times, there is a conflict between **God's Will** and **our will.** You must know that God will move in accordance with His Will and not ours.

When you know the Will of God for your life, it becomes the foundation of prayer which is His Word. Let us look at the life of Elijah, someone who knew the power of prayer. He prayed for rain. He knew that was the Will of God, because while he was in prayer God spoke to him and told him it was going to rain.

Read 1 King 18:41&45 KJV says, "There is a sound of abundance of rain. Verse 45 says, "And it came to pass in the meanwhile, that the heaven was black with clouds and wind, and there was a great rain." This tells me that, when Elijah prayed the Word of God, God heard him and he heard God. (He knew God's voice).

If your relationship with God and your foundation of prayer is solid, you will be able to *stand strong* in these last days and nothing will be able to move you or shake your faith when it is challenged.

Jesus came to do the Will of the Father. The Will of God for Jesus was for Him to give His life so that we could have eternal life. (God's Will is that no one be lost)

John 6:38-40 KJV says, "For I came down from heaven, not to do my own will, but the will of him that sent me. And this is the Father's will which hath sent me, that of all which he hath given me I should lose nothing, but should raise it up again at the last day. And this is the will of him that sent me, that everyone which seeth the Son, and believeth on him, may have everlasting life: and I will raise him up at the last day."

As you and I live in awareness of the presence of God, study and meditate in His

Word, "His Will" is made known to us. We should begin to express God's desires and His thoughts in our prayers. God then becomes a reflection in us.

God wants you to act on His Will, and not to try and figure it out; just as Jesus did. Jesus acted out the Will of God. Not once did we read in the *Bible*, that Jesus had to figure things out. No, **He prayed the Will of God**.

Knowing God's Will (His Word), gives us the confidence we need to go to Him in prayer. It also gives us an assurance that He hears us when we pray. **The knowledge of God's Will is always accompanied by the peace of God.** Ask God for wisdom. What is the Will for your life? Are you at the church He (God) wants you to attend? What is your role in the church? Find out what drives you? What are your interests, gifts? He may reveal His Will in different ways. God may give you a word or maybe an idea concerning His Will for you to act on. His instructions require obedience.

Remember, Jesus did not stop praying for the Will of God to be fulfilled in His life. He continued to pray daily. So, we are not exempt. We must pray daily, for God's Will for our life to be fulfilled.

PLUG IN AND STAY CONNECTED

JESUS went about doing good. He was neither afraid nor intimidated by the people. He was surrounded by the lame, sick, witches, warlocks, psychics, alcoholics, prostitutes, familiar spirits etc...

Jesus knew who he was. He had total confidence in His Father. The Word of God tells us that he sought the Father for direction. Jesus did not doubt in His heart. He knew God's Word would come to pass.

After Jesus spent time with God, then He went out. He never went without seeking

God first. Jesus knew **He was equipped and anointed by God** to destroy the works of the devil. When Jesus recognized evil spirits around, He took authority over them **by speaking the Word of God (only the Word)!** Jesus was not afraid or moved by what He saw. (Surely, He saw some evil things all around Him).

1 John 4:4 KJV says, "Ye are of God, little children, and have overcome them: because greater is He that is in you, than he that is in the world."

God abided in Him and He in the Father (they are one). Jesus had the power and the authority to destroy the strongholds that were holding the people in bondage.

The *Bible* never said Jesus wondered if He could walk among those people, or if the spirits might jump on Him. NO! He kept His eyes on God and Satan had to flee. The demons all trembled and obeyed Him.

Jesus spoke the Word and healing came. He did not have to beg God to heal or deliver the people. Jesus was totally focused on the Will of God for His life. He delivered and set free those who were bound. Jesus was not concerned about what the people would think about Him. This demonstration shows us that we can do the same and greater works than these.

John 14:12 KJV says, "Verily, Verily, I say unto you, He that believeth on me, the works that I do shall he do also; and greater works than these shall he do; because I go unto my Father."

"Speak out" the Word of God with confidence—knowing God will do the work. He will heal the sick and open the blind eyes. Deaf ears will hear, tongues will be loosed and Satan will flee. Not might, but **will** flee.

Jesus never spoke what He thought. He spoke only the words the Father instructed

Him to speak which were words of life. The Word also says that the demons recognized the power and authority of the words Jesus spoke. This teaches us that when we speak the Word of God (with faith) over any situation (sickness, finances, marriages, jobs etc…) it has to obey. This is the authority God intended for our life.

NOTICE: Mark 1:23-26 KJV says, "And there was in their synagogue a man with an unclean spirit; and he cried out, Saying, Let us alone; what have we to do with thee, thou Jesus of Nazareth? Art thou come to destroy us? I know thee who thou art, the Holy One of God. And Jesus rebuked him, saying, **Hold thy peace, and come out of him**. And when the unclean spirit had torn him, and cried with a loud voice, he came out of him."

The demons even recognized that the Word of God is so powerful it came to destroy evil.

Take a little time and meditate on the above mentioned.

1. The unclean spirits **knew who Jesus was,** the Son of the Living God.

2. The unclean spirits **knew why Jesus came,** (to destroy them).

3. The unclean spirits **knew what would happen if Jesus spoke the Word of God out of His mouth.**

    (Demons would have to flee).

    Satan and his demons are afraid of the Power and the Anointing in the Word of God...through the blood of Jesus, in the name of Jesus.

    Connect: Read, study and meditate on the Word of God daily. Speak it out in prayer, just as Jesus did, with the "Authority and Boldness" that has been given to you by God. Know His Word.

This is why I can say with boldness and confidence **PLUG IN AND STAY CONNECTED TO GOD.**

YOUR CONNECTION REQUIRES PRAYERS

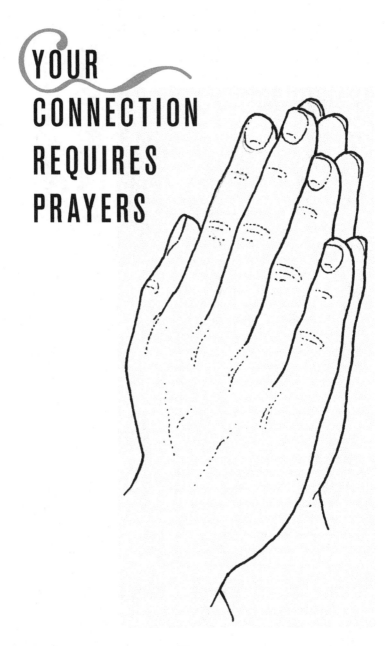

What is **prayer**? What is God's **purpose**? What is God's **plan**? Why are some prayers unanswered?

C━

PRAYER IS... communicating with God and God communicating with you (gives instructions/directions for your life). Prayer helps you to establish an intimate relationship with God. It is a tool to usher in the return of Jesus Christ. Prayer will help you to stand strong in times when you must face your adversities. It will empower you to defeat the enemy. Prayer moves the hand of God. **Prayer is spiritual warfare.** Prayer is not a ritual, it is fellowship with God. It will increase your faith and your love for Him. Prayer also builds intimacy with God. It affirms His purpose and Will for your life. It also brings honor, respect and integrity into your lives. **Prayer has POWER**, power to change, and transform lives (in cities, states, nation and world). It can change circumstances, and give you peace in the midst of any storm you might be facing. Prayer is the key, and faith unlocks the door.

Mark 11:24 KJV says, "Therefore I say unto you, what things so ever ye desire, when you pray, believe that ye receive them, and ye shall have them."

Your prayers must be based on the Word of God.

GOD'S PURPOSE...God is a God of Purpose and Design. Every person was created with a purpose in the mind of God. (We are no accident—we were created for a reason). You cannot fulfill your purpose focusing on yourself. Ask God to reveal His purpose (He is our creator). Knowing your purpose will prepare you for eternal life with God. We were created to fellowship, praise and worship the Father.

Fellowship means...a warm, friendly feeling among people; companionship. Loving one another.

Praise means...words that show high regard and approval of. To worship.

Worship means...prayers, acts done to pay honor to God. To give love or devotion to. Thanksgiving.

John 4:23-24 KJV says, "But the hour cometh, and now is, when the true worshippers shall worship the Father in spirit and in truth: for the Father seeketh such to worship Him. God is a Spirit: and they that worship Him must worship Him in spirit and in truth."

GOD'S PLAN...God's plan for us from the beginning is to **know Him.** We were created to have fellowship with Him and experience His presence and power. He wants us to live an abundant and productive life. His plans for us are good and full of hope. He will be with us to fulfill our destiny that He has for us. (He planned our life for His purpose). He wants to give us the desires of our heart.

Jeremiah 29:11 KJV says, "For I know the thoughts that I think toward you, says the Lord, thoughts of peace, and not of evil, to give you an expected end."

John 10:10 says, "The thief cometh not, but to steal, and to kill, and to destroy: *I am come* that they might have life, and that they might have it more abundantly."

OVERCOMING UNANSWERED PRAYERS:

Some of the hindrances that people experience in their prayer life are;

1. Some people avoid praying because **they do not get immediate results.**

2. They **do not believe** there is **Power in prayer.**

3. There is a **lack of respect for God's Word and interest inside the church.**

4. Some are simply **lazy and make excuses** as to why they do not have time to pray.

5. Some **do not know how to pray.**

6. Some think they are **not worthy** to go to God.

Prayers that are unanswered can sometimes bring **discouragement**. When this happens, we may begin to **doubt** God and His love for us. We do not trust Him and begin to turn to other gods. Some turn to occults, gangs, horoscopes, witchcraft, psychic hot lines (looking for acceptance/answers), etc... We feel rejected, lose hope and **become negative.** We begin to think that our prayers are not answered because we do not have enough faith in God or maybe God does not hear us. We enter into **disbelief** because we think it is something we did, or did not do. Then, **condemnation** comes upon us because we think we are not praying long enough. Satan **torments** our minds and makes us think that answered prayers are just for special people or super-spiritual Christians. We then begin to rely on ourselves, church groups, or other people's beliefs. These spiritual highs and lows can cause emotional **frustrations** because of unanswered prayers. This can be discouraging and depressing in the life of a believer.

C

When your prayers do not bring forth immediate results or manifestation, God may be saying wait, not now. Unanswered prayers can be a good thing too. Think about it, if you got everything you prayed for, it may turn out that it is not good for you or maybe it is too much for you to handle or even to soon (which could destroy you).

Unanswered prayers can also be an indication that there is hidden sin in your life. Ask God what is hindering your prayers. He will tell you or show you why your prayers are not being answered.

James 1:5 KJV says, "If any you lack wisdom, let him ask of God, that give to all men liberally and upbraideth not; and it shall be given to him."

Maybe, you are holding unforgiveness in your heart for someone who offended or hurt you in the past. If so, **repent and forgive them (let it go),** so that your prayers will not be hindered. (Forgiveness is not for the other person, it is actually for you). God asks us to be kind one to another, tenderhearted, forgiving one another even as God for Christ's sake has forgiven you.

As a Christian you must do a self-evaluation.

Ask yourself? Is there sin in my life?

Ask yourself? Is there an open door for Satan to come in and hinder my prayer life?

Ask yourself? Am I praying in line with the Word of God?

Continue to seek God and wait patiently, until you receive the answer from Him.

YOUR CONNECTION REQUIRES FAITHFULNESS

Peter, James, and John went out fishing one day, but they caught no fish, not one. The *Bible* says they were so tired and exhausted from being in the hot sun all day that they gave up and decided to return to shore. After reaching the bank of the shore, Simon heard a voice coming toward him. As he lifted up his head and looked out, he saw Jesus walking up to him saying, "Simon, go back out there into the deep waters and let down your **nets** for a catch."

I could just imagine the look upon Simon's face after being out there all day and not catching anything. Thoughts must have entered into his mind such as, "This man must be kidding; we're hot, tired, and dirty." All we want to do is go home, clean up, eat and rest. Why go out there, what for?

Instead, Simon answered Jesus with "Faith." Luke 5:5 KJV says, "And Simon answering, said unto Him, Master, we have toiled all the night, and have taken nothing: nevertheless at thy word I will let down the net."

This tells me that, in spite of how Simon felt physically or what he might have been thinking mentally, he obeyed Jesus and acted on His word. (He did not murmur or complain).

To have God's best, we must be willing to launch out into the deep (as it relates to our situation or circumstances), even when we don't feel like it. Good examples would be not feeling like going to church or not feeling like going to work. Often times, our miracle or breakthrough is right around the corner, but we give up too soon. *We let our feelings dictate to us what we should be doing.* Then, discouragement sets in when we do not see immediate results (answers to our prayers).

The disciples received a miracle when they **acted in faith and obedience** to the spoken word of Jesus. They received a great multitude of fish, which caused their net to break. This tells me that they had more than enough. They received more than they had room to contain and they received supernatural provision and supernatural abundance. Praise God, their cup was running over!

When God tells us to do something, we often give Him excuses. Who me? Why me? I don't think *I* can do this or that. You may be thinking, *I'm* so busy, *I'm* tired, let someone else do it etc... Excuses, Excuses, Excuses. God does not want to hear your excuses. *God will not ask you to do anything that He knows you are not capable of doing.* He will equip you to do whatever He asks you to do. (Remember, **it is not your ability, but it is His power working through you.**

When Simon Peter returned to Jesus, he realized what was happening around him! He was so overwhelmed, he could not contain himself and fell down at Jesus' feet.

Like many of us, we believe God's Word, but when the manifestation of our prayers takes place in our lives, *it is over whelming to our natural minds.* (Our answered prayers are like a **WOW** moment. Look at God).

What awesome results we get from God by speaking, believing, and acting on the Word.

Faith is the key. Hebrews 11:1 KJV says, "Now faith is the substance of things hoped for, the evidence of things not seen."

Faith requires action. In spite of feeling tired and exhausted, Simon still acted out in Faith and Obedience to Jesus. He believed Him at His word. He did not go by what he saw in the natural.

2 Corinthians 5:7 KJV says, "For we walk by faith and not by sight."

Have faith in God. So, I ask you to put aside your feelings. Do not let your emotions dictate your actions; do what **God** is asking you to do. Do not procrastinate.

YOUR
CONNECTION
REQUIRES
OBEDIENCE

Read Genesis 22:1-17 KJV

Abraham was obedient to God. He was a man of great faith and obedience. *(God will use difficult circumstances to develop your character). He wants to stretch your faith and sharpen your character. He is (God) not trying to take anything away from you. He is trying to get something to you.*

Abraham was at peace with God. He trusted Him at His word. Abraham communed with the Father and, therefore, built an intimate relationship with Him.

One day, God spoke to Abraham and told him to take his son Isaac (whom he loved very much) to the land of Moriah, upon one of the mountains and offer him up as a sacrifice to Him.

Abraham did not question God. He never murmured or complained. Instead, Abraham went to sleep and rested for his journey. Early the next morning, he went out and chopped wood for the fire. (Notice here, he did not sleep in (sleep late), nor did he procrastinate). He saddled up his donkey, took his son Isaac, two of his servants, and he went on.

It took three days before Abraham saw the place of sacrifice. (Surely, being human-Abraham prayed, casting down wicked thoughts and imaginations from his mind as he went up to the land of Moriah. He rebuked Satan and stayed focus). Abraham had obeyed God in other ways.

He learned the importance of obeying God. But this was the hardest, I'm sure. Sometimes God will ask for the very thing that you want to hold on so tightly to.

The Word of God tells us that Abraham told his two servants to wait while he and Isaac went up to worship God. Again, notice he did not take his two servants with him to worship. He did not even tell them or discuss with them what he was about to do. He gave no place to the devil or even for someone to talk him out of doing what God told him to do. This was between him and God. **Sometimes, we have to be quiet when it comes to the things we know God has asked us to do.**

As they went up, Abraham prepared the altar for a burnt offering, just as God asked him to.

Isaac turned and said to his Father, we have everything, but where is the lamb for the sacrifice? Again, Abraham did not discuss this, not even with his son. Abraham said, "**GOD WILL PROVIDE**" (notice, the words that came out of Abraham's mouth. **These were powerful words spoken from his lips**). Abraham continued working. He had confidence and trust in God. He knew that, if God asked him to sacrifice his son, He was well able to raise him (Isaac) from the dead. He believed God in all things.

Genesis 22:9-13 KJV says, "And they came to the place which God had told him of; and Abraham built an altar there, and laid the wood in order, and bound Isaac his son, and laid him on the altar upon the wood. And Abraham stretched forth his hand, and took the knife to slay his son. And the angel of the Lord called unto him out of heaven, and said, **Abraham, Abraham**: and he said, here am I. And he said, Lay not thine hand upon the lad (boy), neither do thou anything unto him: for now I know that thou fearest God, seeing thou has not withheld thy son, thine only son from me. And Abraham lifted up his eyes, and looked, and behold behind him a ram caught in a thicket by his horns: and Abraham went and took the ram, and offered him up for a burnt offering instead of his son."

God was well-pleased, and He blessed Abraham and his descendants because of his obedience.

God really did not want Abraham to kill Isaac. He wanted him to **sacrifice Isaac in his heart** (He tested his faith and obedience). The test was only to strengthen his character. God refines us through our difficult situations. Remember, our trials have not come to destroy us, but to get something to us.

We can learn a lot from this story about Abraham. He demonstrated and acted in faith and obedience. He did not complain.

His obedience brought great rewards to him. He built an intimate relationship/ fellowship with God.

He heard God's voice, and he obeyed God.

Sometimes we ask God, "How can I please you?" When we try to please God in our own way, we fail. Then, Satan comes to bring condemnation to our minds and hearts. We struggle with letting God down. The Word of God in Romans 8:1 KJV says, "There is therefore, now no condemnation to them which are in Christ Jesus."

I found out that we cannot do anything by ourselves. It is not our ability; but it is God's (Holy Spirit) ability working in us. (The Holy Spirit reveals things to us).

With the Holy Spirit working in and through you and I, He (God) is then glorified in the Earth, not we ourselves. (You and I are ONLY THE VESSELS being used by God). God is pleased when we are obedient to Him and **He receives all the Glory, Honor and Praise.**

Like Abraham's challenge, sometime it is difficult to understand what God is trying to accomplish through us and how he chooses to build character in us.

There were times when I have felt inadequate to speak before people and did not understand the call of God on my life.

I often thought, "What if *I* mess up? What if *I* trip? What if *I* fall in front of all those people? What if *I* forget the scriptures and go blank?"

One day the Lord spoke to me and said, "What if, what if, what if, all these what if's—STOP SYLVIA! Think about what thoughts you are allowing in your mind. Stay focused. **This is about Me (God).** All I need you to do is be 'willing and obe-

dient'. I have given you a comforter 'the Holy Spirit' who will be speaking through you. Remember, my Word says in John 14:26 KJV, "But the Comforter, which is the Holy Ghost, whom the Father will send in my name, He shall teach you all things, and bring all things to your remembrance, whatsoever I have said unto you."

All those "what if" thoughts were tormenting my mind. There were some uncertainties of moving under God's directions (at that time of my life). But, God (the Holy Spirit) promises to lead us and guide us in all truth.

So, I made a quality decision that I would do what God wanted me to do, regardless of how I felt, or what I thought. I would do it simply out of obedience to Him. Despite my fear…I was going to obey God.

Let me share one of my personal experiences that may help you, as it did me. I can vividly remember a time when a Pastor called me out of the congregation to come up front and minister to the people who had come up for prayer.

Out of obedience to God, I went up. As I walked to the front, I spoke with the Holy Spirit, "Holy Spirit, have your way with me, and let me decrease as you increase in me. I am a vessel for God; now, Lord, use me for your Glory. **Holy Spirit let me say only what the Father wants me to say** and not what I *think* I should say."

I recall, when I began to pray and yield to the Holy Spirit, the "POWER OF GOD" fell upon me and I felt like someone lifted me up and I was walking on air, in slow motion. I begin to shake with such a vibration; it was like a bolt of electricity hit my body. (This was not an aching pain, like we know pain to be in the natural, but this was an assurance that something good was taking place- something spiritual). As I was praying in the Holy Spirit, one of my arms lifted straight up in the air. (I tried to pull it down, but I couldn't and I realized this had to be God). With my arm lifted in the air, my hand began to wave over the congregation. In the Spirit, I could hear a loud cheering, sweeping through the Body of Christ. The more the Holy Spirit had me to wave my hand and pray in the Spirit, the more it appeared to me (in my natural eyesight) that a fog was slowly moving across the church and the congregation. As the Holy Spirit spoke through me to pray for the people that came up for prayer- I knew that things were happening in the spirit realm (God is a Spirit). I believe that healing and deliverance was taking place. Whatever was needed in the lives of the people, they received it as the anointing removed burdens and destroyed yokes.

I also believed, when the Power of God fell upon us, **we were in unity- with one mind and in one accord**. God was able to move by His Spirit throughout the Body of Christ. There was oneness and wholeness, lifting up that name above every name Jesus Christ, the Son of the Living God.

When I finished praying, I returned to my seat, thanking the Holy Spirit for speaking through me. I remember saying to the Lord, "Lord, I hope I acted in obedience to everything you wanted me to do, **but more than anything God, that you were glorified**."

I can now say I understand why Jesus told the disciples, "I must go, but I will send you a Comforter, the Holy Spirit." He is a person, connected through the Spirit of God, to reveal all truth.

John 16:13 says, "Howbeit when he, the Spirit of truth, is come, he will guide you into all truth: for he shall not speak of himself; but whatsoever he shall hear, that shall he speak: and he will show you things to come."

Now, I know the answer to, "How can I please God?"(Faith with "action" and obedience).

This experience shows how God moves when we act in obedience to Him. I encourage you to surrender/die to self. Be willing and obedient to the things God ask you to do. Trust Him and have faith with action. Ask God to fill you with His Holy Spirit. And allow the Holy Spirit to lead and guide you. **God wants to use all of you for His Glory**.

Can God trust YOU to be Obedient?

BE PERSISTENT IN PURSUING GOD

Drawn by Fred. J. Shields.

Engraved by SWAIN.

P lugging in to God requires persistent faith and determination. There was a woman from Canaan who had a daughter possessed by a demon, and she was constantly tormented. She went to Jesus for help. The disciples did not want her around, and Jesus rejected her. He told her He came for the Jews and not the Gentiles.

She was not offended, nor was she moved by what He said or what the disciples said. She did not stop there. She was determined and knew *why she went to see Jesus and what she wanted Him to do for her daughter.* She pleaded with Jesus and began to worship Him. Jesus was astonished and marveled at her faith and her daughter was totally healed. She was **Persistent** and did not give in or give up. She took a step of faith.

Hebrew 11:1 KJV says, "Now faith is the substance of things hoped for, the evidence (proof) of things not seen."

The woman could have gotten offended three times, because of what Jesus did.

1. Jesus did not answer her.

2. When Jesus finally answered her, he said, I am not sent but unto the lost sheep of the house of Israel.

3. Jesus also told her it is not meant to take the children's bread, and to cast it to the dogs.

She was so persistent, she said to Jesus, "Even the dogs eat of the crumbs, which fall from the masters' table."

Being Persistent will also require you to know God and know who you are in Christ (not just about Him). Pray without doubting in your heart. When you experience adversities or closed doors in your life, do not stop there. **Don't give up!** I believe when one door closes, God will open up a new one. There will be times when you will feel like giving up, or God will ask you to do something that does not make sense—it is out of the ordinary. Be persistent, and just do it. People may criticize you for believing God for something that has not yet manifested in the natural. Resist and withstand the attacks of the devil. When you are in prayer, Satan will also try to come against your mind and bring the spirit of doubt to steal the answer to your prayers (be persistent and cast down thoughts and wicked

imaginations). Satan knows, if doubt dom-
inates your mind, you will not be able to
pray the prayer of faith because **doubt can-
cels faith**.

Matthew 21:21-22 KJV says, "Jesus answered and said unto them, verily I say
unto you, **if you have faith, and doubt not**,
you shall not only do this which is done to
the fig tree, but also if you shall say unto
this mountain, be thou removed, and be
thou cast into the sea; it shall be done. And
all things, whatsoever you shall ask in
prayer, believing, you shall receive."

Be determined and stay focused; do not
give up. **Faith that does not doubt can
produce great results.** You may also come
up against several road blocks, but keep
pursing God and pushing forward. Have
a made up mind, like the woman from Canaan, and know what you want and go
after it with faith in God. You can do all

things with the POWER and AUTHORITY that have been given to you by God.

Hebrew 11:6 KJV says, "But without faith it is impossible to please him; for he that cometh to God must believe that He is, and that He is a rewarder of them that diligently seek Him."

When you pray to God, you must have faith that God will answer your prayers according to His Word.

C~

TO PURSUE GOD means... to capture, to follow, or carry out. You have to discipline your life. Live a life of prayer, fasting and fellowship with God, so He will reveal Himself to you. Your daily strength will come from being connected to the vine.

John 15:4 KJV says, "Abide in Me, and I in you. As the branch cannot bear fruit of itself, except it abide in the vine; no more can ye, except ye abide in me."

Let us look at Jesus' life when He came down in the flesh. Many times, Jesus withdrew Himself from the disciples and sought God in solitude. He needed to know God's directions and God's Will for His life to be fulfilled. Each time Jesus sought God, He was strengthened, empowered, and prepared to defeat Satan (the enemy), with the power of the Word. Jesus knew Satan's characteristics. Jesus also knew who He (Jesus) was in God. Jesus did not face a problem, and then go to God. No, **He always spent time with God BEFORE he faced the enemy.** He was fully armed and ready at all times with the Word of God. (I AM NOT SAYING DON'T TAKE YOUR PROBLEMS TO GOD. YES, TAKE **ALL** THINGS TO GOD IN PRAYER. **PRAY THE ANSWER TO YOUR PROBLEM**). I'm only giving you an illustration of what Jesus did beforehand. He is our example.

We must allow the Word of God to become the final authority in every area of our lives. We must stay focused and ready at all times, so Satan will not be able to catch us off guard.

1 Peter 5:8 KJV says, "Be sober, be vigilant; because your adversary the devil, as a roaring lion, walking about, seeking whom he may devour."

Do not be distracted by circumstances that may come into your life. **Choose to be persistent and pursue the things of God with faith in Him. Set your heart and mind to seek Him daily.** God has already given us everything we need in life (because of the blood of Jesus). **It is up to us to pursue the things of God.** Even when we get off track, we must seek to find our way back to God and His Word. Remember, there is not anything that can stop you, except you. Be persistent and pursue God.